Burying the Bishop

Burying the Bishop

The funny side of Church life

David Pytches

eagle

Guildford, Surrey

British Library Cataloguing in Publication Data. A catalogue record for this book is available from the British Library.

Published by Eagle, an imprint of Inter Publishing Service (IPS) Ltd, PO Box 530, Guildford, Surrey GU2 5FH.

Typeset by Eagle
Printed by Cox & Wyman
ISBN No: 0 86347 302 4

This book is dedicated to my good friend
George Knight.
For his inspiring Christian faith and his
irrepressible sense of humour.
'There was corn in Egypt'

CONTENTS

INTRODUCTION

I remember the delightful shock I had when I first read Hesketh Pearson's *Smith of Smiths*. It was a life of the nineteenth-century clergyman, Canon Sydney Smith, a social reformer and vintage conversationalist. His humour was tear-jerking and side-splitting.

Thomas Carlyle called him 'a fellow of infinite fun'. George III remarked that he was 'a very clever fellow but would never be a bishop', which prompted Smith to quip that his natural brother (Bobo) had risen by his gravity whilst he himself had sunk through his levity! Daniel O'Connor called him 'The ancient and amusing defender of the faith'. Lord Cochrane wrote, 'Was there ever more sense combined with more hilarious jocularity?' Sir Henry Holland was of the opinion that the power and diversity of Sydney Smith's wit was greater than that of any man he had ever known. Charles Dickens never met him but expressed the greatest curiosity to see and the greatest interest to know him. Thomas Moore wrote, 'Sydney Smith at breakfast made me actually cry with laughter. I was obliged to start up from the table.' Queen Victoria used to go into fits of laughter at the sayings of Sydney Smith, which were repeated to her by her prime minister, Lord Melbourne.

Why do I make so much of Sydney Smith?
Often good books like Law's *Serious Call* made
me feel guilty about dwelling on the funny
side of life. After all I might well be ending up
as a missionary. Even though Sydney Smith
mocked such a calling, nevertheless his mirth
released me and did not deter me. I began to
realise the great value of a sense of humour in
life. I discovered later that missionaries were
advised to have a strong sense of humour and
a weak sense of smell. Though we always take
God very seriously we should never take ourselves too seriously. People and real-life situa-
tions can be very funny and God has given us
a sense of humour to enjoy each other. The
Bible is approving when it says, 'A merry
heart doeth good like a medicine' (Poverbs
17:22).

People who laugh often live longer.
Humour is also a wonderful tool for breaking
tensions. It helps sometimes to make a sermon
point in a humorous fashion if the telling of
jokes happens to be one's gift, but it's very
counterproductive if it's not. The timing and
precision of the punch line is vital. 'If you can't
remember them don't dismember them!' is
valuable advice here. In reaching outsiders for
the Kingdom of God it is also useful. Some fish
can be easily caught if they are tickled. Finally,
according to Baron von Hugel, one test for the
canonising of a saint is that he or she must
have had a sense of humour.

Oscar Wilde once heard James Whistler saying something very funny and Wilde muttered admiringly, 'Gosh, I wish I had said that,' to which came Whistler's prompt response, 'You will, Oscar, you will.'

It is said that if you steal from one author it's plagiarism; if you steal from two or three it's literary discernment; if you steal from many it is thorough research. In my 'thorough research' for this collection I gratefully acknowledge indebtedness to *Frogs in Cream* by Steve Gaukroger and Nick Mercer, and *Bishop's Brew* by Ronald Brow (bishop of Birkenhead). I have no idea where most of the other wit first originated. Where there is no acknowledgement I can only beg forgiveness if unintentionally I have caused hurt, or given offence, through repeating any of these jokes recorded here. There is inevitably something risky about a joke and there can be no guarantee that someone will not misunderstand it. One man's meat is another man's poison.

David Pytches
June 1999

One

ATHEISTS, AGNOSTICS
AND DOUBTERS

They have all sorts of new services today. Now they've got a dial-a-prayer service for atheists. You call a number and nobody answers.

The atheists of America have just announced that they will hold their annual convention on April 17th. God willing!

Sign on the tomb of an atheist:
HERE LIES AN ATHEIST
ALL DRESSED UP
AND NO PLACE TO GO.

Verger's advice to visiting preacher: 'You'll 'ave to shout very loud in this 'ere church vicar. The agnostics are somefink terrable!'

Some are atheists only in fair weather.

Thank God I'm an atheist.
(Luis Bunuel)

I was an atheist until I realised I was God.

An atheist has no invisible means of support

I have spent a lot of time searching the Bible for loopholes.
(W.C. Fields)

I used to be indecisive but now I'm not so sure.

(Boscoe Pertwee)

The vicar was very ill and was told by his doctor not to have too many visitors. However, when his agnostic friend called, the unbeliever was ushered in to the vicar's bedside.

'I do appreciate,' said the agnostic, 'your seeing me when so many of your friends have not been permitted to come.' 'Well, its like this,' said the vicar, 'I feel confident that I shall see my friends in heaven, but I was worried that this might be my last chance to see you!'

I don't know what's happening to this world. I saw a long skinny insect standing like this (arms crossed) and I said: 'Aren't you a praying mantis?' and he said 'No, I'm an agnostic.'

Christianity will go. It will vanish and shrink. I needn't argue about that. I'm right and I'll be proved right. We're more popular than Jesus now! *(words spoken by John Lennon who then had to withdraw his remark when the Beatles toured the USA)*

Have you heard about the agnostic, dyslexic, insomniac who lay awake at night wondering: 'Is there a Dog?'

Some people say there is a God; others say there is no God. The truth probably lies somewhere in between. *(W.B. Yeats)*

It is hard to see how a great man can be an atheist. Doubters do not believe. Sceptics do not contribute. Cynics do not create. Faith is the great motive power, and no man realises his full possibilities unless he has the deep conviction that life is eternally important, and that his work, well done, is part of an unending plan.

My dear child, you must believe in God – in spite of what the clergy tell you.

(Margot Asquith)

Two

BIBLE CHARACTERS

Q: At what time of day was Adam born?
A: A little before Eve.

Teacher: Why was Adam a famous runner?
Student: Because he was in the first human race.

Q: Who is the smallest man in the Bible?
A: Some people believe that it was Zacchaeus. Others believe it was Bildad, the Shuhite. But in reality it was Peter, the disciple – he slept on his watch!

Q: Who was the most popular actor in the Bible?
A: Samson. He brought the house down.

Q: Who was the straightest man in the Bible?
A: Joseph. Pharaoh made a ruler out of him.

Ned: What instructions did Noah give his sons about fishing off the ark?
Fred: I don't know.
Ned: Go easy on the bait, boys. I only have two worms.

Q: What animal took the most baggage into the ark?
A: The elephant. He took his trunk, while the fox and the rooster only took a brush and comb.

Q: What man in the Bible had no parents?
A: Joshua, the son of Nun.

Q: What did Jonah do for three days in the belly of the big fish?
A: Sang, of course! Everybody sings in Wales!

Q: What sort of lighting did Noah have on the ark?
A: No, not arc lighting – flood lighting.

Q: Where do professors come from?
A: From the West. Because the wise men came from the East.

Eve: Adam, do you love me?
Adam: Who else?

Adam was created first . . . to give him a chance to say something.

And God said to Noah: 'Will you build me an ark?'
    'Yes, Lord. You know that I will. But there's just one question, Lord.'
    'Yes, Noah?'
    'What's an ark?'

A wise guy stopped a bus the other morning and said to the driver, 'Well, Noah, you got here at last. Is the ark full?'
    Replied the driver, 'Not quite. We need one more monkey. Come on in.'

Said Daniel, entering the lions' den: 'Well, whoever does the after-dinner speaking, it won't be me!'

Talk of the patience of Job, said a hospital nurse, Job was never on night duty. *(Stephen Paget)*

It was a Rotarian who was the first man to call John the Baptist Jack.

An epistle is the wife of an apostle.

Exasperated housewife: 'Why didn't Noah swat those two flies when he had the chance?'

Cain was a juvenile delinquent without being born on the wrong side of the tracks.

Professionals built the Titanic; amateurs built the ark.

Adam ate the forbidden fruit but he blamed it on Eve. Eve blamed it on the serpent and the serpent didn't have a leg to stand on.

The Bible tells us to love our neighbours, and also to love our enemies; probably because they are generally the same people. *(G.K. Chesterton)*

Three

BISHOPS

A bishop was having to speak on the same subject in several different areas of his diocese. He would begin his address by welcoming any members of the press who might be present but then added how much he would appreciate it if they would not repeat his jokes in their write-ups as he wanted to tell the jokes again at his next meeting. The press were very obliging. One of them gave a factual account of the bishop's address and added that he also told a number of jokes which can't be repeated!

A recent bishop of Norwich was told the only way to lead the Norfolk people was first of all to find out which way they were going and then walk in front of them.

Efforts are being made to improve the efficiency of our bishops. They are now being issued with in-trays marked sacred and top sacred.

A bishop of London was seated next to the French Ambassador when a fly settled on the tablecloth. Although the conversation had been in English, the bishop was keen to show off his knowledge of French in the presence of the ambassador. 'Le mouche,' he commented, airily. After a brief glance, the Ambassador smiled and said, 'La mouche.' The bishop studied the insect once again very closely and finally he exclaimed, 'I must say you've got remarkably good eyesight!'

The bishop of Aberdeen and the Orkneys complained to one of his clergy about the way he had been addressed in a letter: 'I know it was the festive season but I can assure you that I wasn't that bad when I visited your church at Christmas'; and he returned the letter addressed to the Tight Reverend F. Darwent. (*Church Times* 20/1/89)

Bishop John Austin Baker was warmly shaken by the hand of an American visitor to Westminster Abbey after he had preached there. The visitor commented: 'Father, all the time you were talking, I had the strongest feeling that you were trying to tell us something!'

Robert Runcie, one-time Archbishop of Canterbury used to tell the following story of when he was the Bishop of St Albans. On his way by car to an evening meeting, he saw some splendid hams hanging in the butcher's shop of a village high street he was passing through. His driver stopped the car and hurried in to buy one before the shop closed.

The bishop followed close behind and was just in time to hear the butcher telling the driver: 'Yes, certainly the bishop can have a ham with pleasure, and if he can get rid of our present vicar, he can have the whole d— pig!

A former bishop of Exeter was renowned for his bad memory. On one occasion he was travelling by train to a certain part of his diocese. Before he reached his destination, the ticket collector appeared demanding to see all tickets. The bishop groped his way through this pockets but no ticket could be found. Finally the ticket collector lost patience and said: 'Tha's o' right bishop. We all know you's an harnest man. It don't matter!' 'Oh indeed it does!' replied the bishop. 'Without that ticket I shan't know where to get off this train!'

A bishop had a dream that he was preaching in St Paul's Cathedral and when he woke up he was!

Archbishop Lang, when rector of Portsea, scandalised his parishioners by walking from the rectory to the church in his cassock. Word went round the parish that the rector was committing celebacy openly in the streets!

A bishop, a scout and the Brain of Britain were aboard a plane whose engine had caught fire. The pilot announced that there were only three parachutes between the four of them and that he needed one of them to report the accident. The Brain of Britain immediately announced that he must have one also as he still had a great contribution to make to life in Britain. He and the pilot baled out pronto.

'My son,' said the bishop to the scout, 'I've had a long life while yours still lies ahead. Take the last parachute and good luck.' 'It's OK,' said the scout, 'there's one left for each of us. The Brain of Britain took my knapsack!'

A bishop was addressing the students at Yale and used the acrostic Y A L E as a framework for a rather uninspiring talk. Filing out at the end of the assembly one student muttered thankfully 'What luck we're not the Massachusetts Institute of Technology!'

I am increasingly convinced that the *Church Times* is now edited by the Devil in person.
(Bishop Gore)

Dean: I can't understand you, bishop. You have a first class chaplain and yet you are always complaining about him to everybody you meet!
Bishop: But of course. Do you think I want to lose him?

A rather ineffective vicar was asked by his bishop what had induced him to enter the ministry. 'I was called,' the vicar replied simply. 'Are you sure,' pondered the bishop, 'that it was not some other voice you heard?'

Instructions have been circulated to all dioceses to the effect that in future all deceased bishops are to be buried 12 feet under instead of the usual 6. The rationale for this is that deep down bishops are really quite nice people.

First friend: It took me forty years to discover I had not the gifts for Holy Orders.
Second friend: Goodness, whatever did you do when you found out?
First friend: It was too late to do anything. By then I was a bishop!

A former bishop of Southwark would take his dog out daily for a walk and was regularly passed by another man walking in the opposite direction. He always had some pessimistic comment to make – usually about the weather. One simply glorious morning the bishop was just wondering if he would meet the man that day and if so what he might say in view of the sunshine? And behold there he was coming into view. As they passed the man looked up: 'Good morning bishop! What a terrible day it was yesterday!'

A former bishop of Gloucester had a defective memory and on one celebrated occasion was walking round a garden party at his home greeting the clergy.

'My dear fellow,' he said to one clergyman, 'how lovely to see you here today; and how is your dear wife?' The clergyman, rather surprised, replied, 'She's dead, my Lord. Don't you remember, you wrote me a very helpful letter at the time?' 'I am sorry,' the bishop exclaimed, 'do, please forgive me.' He moved on.

Later that afternoon the bishop came across the same man again. 'Hello,' he exclaimed, 'good to have you with us and how is your dear wife?' 'Still dead, my Lord,' said the priest, 'still dead.'

The sudden illness of an incumbent necessitated a telegram to the bishop. In the emergency, the bishop came and took the service himself. Afterwards, two very much over-awed churchwardens felt that they must express their thanks, which they did in the following words: 'My Lord, we greatly appreciate your kindness in coming to us; a poorer preacher would have done, but we couldn't find one.'

A bishop of Bath and Wells was visiting a psychiatric hospital in his diocese one afternoon. An inmate was feeling sociable and asked him who he was?
Bishop: I'm the Bishop of Bath and Wells.
Inmate: No! No! Who are you really?
Bishop, insisting: Yes I really am the Bishop of Bath and Wells.
Inmate: Oh well! You'll change after you have been here a while. When I first came here I thought I was Napoleon Bonaparte!

Handley Moule, the saintly bishop of Durham was watching a football match when a goal was scored by the home team. Tossing his silk hat into the air the gaitered bishop cheered: 'Ooooh, what an abundantly blessed goal!'

A bishop was greeting his guests at a garden party when he overheard a new young curate confessing to his friends that he had spent the best years of his life in the arms of another man's wife!

The bishop was scandalised and was about to rebuke the curate when he added: 'Yes, my mother's!' His friends all roared with laughter and the bishop was also very amused.

He moved on to a group of more senior clergy to try the joke out on them. Apropos of nothing he broke into their conversation and said simply: 'Do you know, brethren, I spent the best years of my life in the arms of another man's wife?'

The clergy were duly shocked, as he had himself been moments earlier, and they stared at the bishop aghast. The bishop suddenly began to look very embarrassed: 'Oh dear,' he stammered, 'I've forgotten who it was now!'

The bishop had preached at Harvest Festival and as he stood at the door, people were very complimentary about his sermon. 'Splendid,' said one: 'Thank you for the wonderful message,' said another, and so it went on.

However, one rather shabbily dressed man took the bishop's hand and muttered, 'Pathetic!' before moving out. The compliments started again, but after a few minutes the strange man was back in the queue. This time he said to the bishop, 'Very, very boring,' and again went through the door. The pattern repeated itself yet again. This time the message was, 'Hope you will not be visiting us again too soon!'

Finally everyone had gone except a church-warden. 'Who was that strange man?' asked the bishop. 'He said very peculiar things.' 'Don't worry about him,' came the reply, 'he's a very dear man but a bit simple and he just wanders round repeating what he hears others saying.'

A bishop, invited to a 'county' dinner was surprised not to be offered anything to drink and eventually appealed to his very beautiful hostess: 'Do you think I could have a drop of wine?'

The lady threw up her hands in horror and replied: 'Oh Bishop I am sorry! I thought you were chairman of the Church of England Temperance Society.'

'Not at all,' said the bishop, 'but I am the chairman of the Anti-Porn campaign.'

'Oh!' came the reply, 'I knew there was something I could not offer you.'

The bishop was disappointed with the attendance at the church he was visiting and asked the incumbent if he had advertised the visit. 'No, bishop!' he replied promptly, 'but I'll kill the wretch who did!'

Bishop Henry Montgomery Campbell of London used to say he hated meetings of all kinds. 'Waste of time,' he would snort. On one occasion, he went into a Board of Finance meeting intoning: 'We brought nothing into this meeting and its certain we can carry nothing out.' But then he brightened up a bit – 'Must admit I've had a good day today,' he said. 'Really enjoyed it – I've been out of the diocese to bury a vicar.'

The bishop was preaching his heart out, but was concerned that because of the acoustics people were finding it difficult to hear him. 'Can you all hear me?' he stopped to ask. 'I can,' came a voice near the front, 'but I don't mind exchanging with someone who can't.'

Michael Ramsey, when a canon of Durham Cathedral, locked two American soldiers inside the cathedral one evening and promised to come and let them out in half an hour. Unfortunately he forgot to come!

A Roman Catholic bishop was saying mass in a parish church in his diocese and at the end of the service a woman came forward for prayer: 'Could you pray for me, bishop, please? I've been married for several years now and we would dearly love to have a baby and there is no sign of one yet.' 'Oh! I'd love to,' said the bishop cheerfully, and proceeded to lay hands on her and pray. When he had finished he added: 'I'll be off to Rome tomorrow and when I'm there I'll light a candle for you.' With that he was gone.

Some years later he found himself back in the same area and learnt from the parish priest that the lady now had a family, so he decided to visit her in her home, where he was greeted by the woman surrounded by her seven children. The bishop was delighted for her and asked to see her husband. 'Oh, he's away just now, bishop. Actually he's gone to Rome to see if he can find the candle and blow it out.'

When Bishop of Lewes, the Right Rev Peter Ball was driving along a country lane one night, an approaching car hit the verge, flew over the hedge and landed on its side. The bishop stopped, shone his headlights on the wreckage and approached it to see what help he could give.

A voice from within called: 'Can you get something to break the window so that I can get out?'

The bishop went back to his car and returned with his crook, by which time the driver had managed to free himself.

'There I was in my monastic grey robe, walking towards him with my crook. I must have looked quite a sight with the car headlights shining behind me,' said the bishop. 'When the driver saw me he turned ashen white.'

More shaken by this celestial apparition than by his accident, the driver managed to whisper: 'Where am I and who are you?'

'I think he was quite convinced he must be in heaven,' said the bishop. 'I did not like to tell him my name was Peter. That might have finished him off altogether!' (*Reproduced from* The Times)

A bishop was taking his morning stroll through the woods with his dog when he spotted a corked bottle shaking mysteriously on the ground. He picked it up and heard a little genie inside crying, 'Let me out! Let me out!' When he opened the bottle the genie emerged and expressed extreme relief to be free. 'Bishop, I must grant you a wish. What can I do for you? Give me a challenge?'

The bishop considered this unexpected offer for a moment and then pointed to his rather dilapidated pet dog: 'I have always wanted to enter my dog for the races – could you possibly turn it into a racing hound for me?' The genie looked at the dog and said: 'Well that's not an easy request – there's not really enough to work on! Why don't you ask me for something else?'

So the bishop thought again and suddenly remembered a dreaded sermon he had to preach in Canterbury Cathedral. 'Look!' he said, 'I have always been a hopeless preacher and I wonder if you could possibly help me to preach a good sermon?'

The genie considered this new request carefully but added: 'I think I'd better just take a second look at that dog!'

Bishop, observing his guest at breakfast looking at his boiled egg slightly puzzled:
'I'm afraid you've got a bad egg, Mr Jones!'
Curate discreetly: 'Oh no, my Lord, I assure you, parts of it are excellent.'

Episcopal subtleties to persuade another bishop to take into his diocese a priest who is not altogether satisfactory, are not unknown. This is a practice known in the trade as 'Throwing dead cats over the garden fence'.

For instance, one bone-idle curate is commended in this way – 'Any vicar who gets this young man to work with him will be extremely fortunate.'

A priest, who is too mean to give anyone even a cup of tea, gets a push with, 'A man of rare gifts'.

A crackpot priest is described as 'well-balanced'! The bishop answers the quizzical look of his secretary with, 'Well, that man has chips on *both* shoulders!'

Sometimes, when their patience was exhausted, bishops could be more explicit:

Bill Smith believes that his last parish made him a scapegoat as did his three previous parishes.

Mr Jones left his last curacy because the vicar wanted him to be present at the 9.30 am daily eucharist. He complained that he couldn't work under those conditions!

Mr Brown would be out of his depth in a church car park puddle.

The Revd Ms Green has delusions of adequacy.

Jim Wright sets low personal standards for himself and then consistently fails to achieve them.

Mr Garrett has reached rock bottom and has started to dig!

His archdeacon says he is not so much of a has-been, but more of a won't be.

His last parish would follow him anywhere – but only out of morbid curiosity.

A Welsh priest writes: Bishop Victor Whitsey once asked a Welsh priest to book a meeting with him. It was to be on a Saturday afternoon about six weeks away and he excused himself saying: 'I'm terribly sorry, my Lord, I cannot go, I have a funeral.' 'A funeral!' the bishop exclaimed. 'What do you mean? It's six weeks away.' 'I know,' he said, 'but I am hoping to bury fifteen Englishmen at Twickenham!'

A Naval officer was once detailed to welcome a visiting bishop and escort him round the ship. Being somewhat unused to such instructions and having no idea how to address his special guest, he stood nervously awaiting the bishop's arrival. At last the moment came and the bishop came aboard. There was an uneasy silence before the bishop boomed: 'The Lord be with you!'

This completely baffled the embarrassed officer who was ignorant of any proper response. He hastily ushered the bishop into the ship's chapel which he imagined would be the most appropriate venue for a bishop. 'Tell me,' demanded the bishop as they reached the entrance, 'has this chapel been consecrated?'

'No, bishop,' the officer replied, relieved at last that he could answer a straight question sensibly, 'but we have just had it distempered!'

A Roman Catholic bishop was being interviewed on his appointment to a new diocese. Someone enquired why the bishop wore a ring. He explained that it was a sign that he was married to his diocese. Quick as a shot came the next question: 'Do you believe in divorce?'

A bishop of Manchester once gave his bachelor curates some advice about finding the right kind of wife. He said, 'Find a woman who is pretty, prudent and with private means, and make sure these are in reverse order of importance!'

A bishop, when at Guildford, allowed his palace to be used as a retreat house for the selection of ordination candidates. The candidates were not allowed off the premises and the bishop was surprised to find one of them coming out of the main gate one afternoon as he was coming in. He enquired what the young man was up to. The candidate explained that he had felt led by the Holy Spirit to go into town and do some shopping. 'Oh,' said the bishop, 'what a pity the Holy Spirit didn't tell you also that its early closing for all the shops this afternoon.'

Earlier in the century, a bishop was invited to dinner at Sandringham and was seated beside the old Queen. He was slightly puzzled when she extracted a bit of meat from her own mouth and pressed it into the bishop's hand, muttering something which he didn't quite catch. Unused to palace etiquette he assumed that such a choice morsel from the royal mouth must be a mark of singular favour so he dutifully popped it into his own mouth to chew. It was much harder going than he had imagined and proved very difficult to swallow but finally he got it down. He was very embarrassed a few minutes later when the Queen enquired if her dog, looking up appealingly at the bishop from the floor beside him, had enjoyed the meat?

When Walter Frere was bishop of Truro, a vicar thoughtfully invited him to stay the night after a Confirmation because the weather was very bad. Frere was later making his way along a dimly-lit passage to the vicarage bathroom ,before the evening meal, when the vicar's wife, coming up from behind him, clouted his ear sharply, remarking: 'That'll teach you to ask the bishop to stay without talking to me about it first!'

When William Greer was retiring from the See of Manchester, he said that although he would miss many things there was one aspect of his life which would be improved by laying down the burden of office. 'For years,' he confessed, 'I have found it embarrassing to sign an hotel register with the names "William Manchester" and "Marigold Greer".'

The bishop was the dinner guest. The table was beautifully prepared and the food looked delicious. They were ready to begin. The hostess spoke to her daughter, aged six. 'Mary, will you say Grace, please.' A rather long delay ensued. The mother coaxed the little girl, 'Come on, Mary say what you heard me say this morning at breakfast.' In a loud voice it came out, 'O God, why ever did I invite that bishop to dinner tonight?'

A bishop of Carlisle was terminating an interview with a very difficult woman of the diocese who was calling, once again, at Rose Castle to lodge a complaint about something or other. They were in the hall, getting round to the final handshake, when a secretary went out slamming the door. The bishop's wife called downstairs: 'Has that stupid woman finally gone dear?' Quick as a flash, the bishop replied, 'O yes, my love, she went ages ago. I'm with Mrs Robinson now.'

One bishop greeting another
bishop in the dole queue: 'A
long time no See.'

A priest was transferred to a diocese whose
bishop was renowned for being very strict
and disciplinarian. His parish priest greeted
him with the words: 'Welcome to the Cruel
See . . .'

A bishop went to the barber. He had precisely three hairs left on his head.

'I want a shampoo and blow-dry, please,' he said.

'Very good, sir,' said the barber slightly flummoxed.

After all was washed and dried, the barber enquired – 'On which side shall I part it, sir?'

'On the left side, please.'

After a moment's consternation – 'I'm very sorry, sir, but one of your hairs has come out.'

'Oh, that's all right. Part it in the middle.'

After another moment of anguish: 'I'm frightfully sorry, sir, but another one has come out.'

'Then don't worry,' said the bishop, 'just leave it rough!'

A bishop called all the clergymen in his diocese together. 'I've got some good news and some bad news,' he told them. 'The good news is I spoke to God the other day and everything's OK. The bad news is She called me from Salt Lake City.'

A clergyman phoned his rural dean: 'I regret to have to inform you that my wife has just died. Could you please send a substitute for the weekend?'

A High Church bishop once found his mitre needed reversing during the service, having been placed on his head back to front. A server realised the predicament and started to turn it round for the bishop. 'Steady on there, lad,' said the bishop, 'it doesn't screw on, you know.'

A former bishop of Reading was taking tea in a country vicarage prior to an evening Confirmation service. The vicar's wife was engaged preparing the tea in the kitchen when the phone went in the vicar's study. Excusing himself to answer it, the vicar left his little daughter to entertain the bishop while he was in the study. Seizing the opportunity, the little girl asked the bishop if he could solve a question her father said he could never understand? The bishop smiled and said he'd have a try. 'Well,' said the little girl innocently, 'my father says he could never understand how you were made a bishop!'

What a blonde – she was enough to make a bishop kick a hole in a stained-glass window.
(Raymond Chandler)

It was once reported in *Private Eye* that the bishops were met together in conclave when they received notice that the Holy Spirit had resigned from the Church of England! 'Whatever are we going to do now?' bemoaned a couple of new bishops. A wise old hand soon calmed them down: 'We shall just carry on as usual, of course!'

Four

CHURCH NOTICE BOARDS, ANNOUNCEMENTS AND MAGAZINES

A church notice board:
'Don't keep the faith –
spread it around.'

Mrs Thomas wishes to thank all
those members who so kindly
assisted in the death of her husband.

Advertisement for a grave digger at
a country church graveyard:
'Good opening for elderly man.'

The regular Monday night choir practice will be held on Tuesday night instead of Friday night.

'I am sorry to announce that our minister is ill. I am here to take his place. I will do the best I can. As you know I am not a minister. I am an undertaker!'

From a diocesan news sheet: 'You will all be pleased to hear that the bishop is making very slow progress after his operation.'

Mr Timms, who was excommunicated from this church on account of dancing is now back with us again in good standing.

Church announcement: 'Would the person who left his chewing gum stuck to the underside of the front pew last Sunday please collect it from the verger afterwards who has kindly kept it in working order!'

A notice stuck to the automatic hot-air hand dryer in the men's toilet at church had these words on it: 'Press this button for free repeat of last Sunday's sermon!'

Tuesday at 4:00 pm there will be an ice cream social. Ladies giving milk should come early.

In view of the popularity of the church ladies annual outing it has been decided to hold it twice a year. *(Sussex parish magazine)*

The new loudspeaker system installed in the church has been given by Mr Jones in memory of his wife.

Please don't walk on church lawn. Grass grows by the inch but is worn down by the foot!

For those who have children and don't know it, we have a creche and nursery in the crypt.

Remember in prayer the many who are sick both of our church and the community.

Many are cold but few are frozen.

Life is not always what you want
but it's what you get.

Notice in cemetery: 'Any day above
ground is a good one.'

You don't stop laughing because
you grow old: you grow old
because you stop laughing.

Despite growing inflation,
the wages of sin remain
absolutely the same.

Report of a church meeting: The
rector spoke briefly and delighted
the audience.

Don't let worry kill you.
Let the Church help!

Next Sunday is 'Giving Sunday'. This church is so sacrificial in its giving that we are in an irreversible trend – but that could change.

Smile at someone who you find hard to love. Say 'hell ' to someone who doesn't care much about you.

Next Sunday Mrs Brown will sing a solo at the morning service before the vicar preaches on the subject of 'Terrible experiences and how to survive them'.

Colin Thompson and Jessica Brown were married on October 26th in the church. So ends a friendship that began in their schooldays!

The ladies of the church have cast off clothing of every kind and they may be seen in the basement on Saturday morning.

Weight Watchers will meet at 7 pm next Wednesday in the church lounge. Please use large double door at the side entrance.

Pot Luck Supper:
Prayer and medication will follow.

From a Church Service Sheet:
Solo: Death where is thy sting?
Hymn: Search me, O God.

The organist invites any members of the congregation who enjoy sinning to volunteer for the choir.

Ladies are requested not to have children in the church kitchen.

Players picked for St. Andrew's darts team will be pinned to this board on Thursday.

Next Sunday is the vicar's last. Special Anthem: 'Come ye thankful people come.'

Lost dog: Has three legs, blind in left eye, right ear missing, broken tail, no teeth, recently castrated. Responds to the name of *Lucky.*

Did you hear about the man who took his car in for a service but couldn't get it through the church door?

The vicar had been in hospital for several weeks undergoing routine surgery and at last he was able to ask his churchwardens to let his parishioners know he was on the road to recovery. The next day people read the following announcement on the Church Notice Board: 'God is good. The vicar is better.'

From parish magazine: 'Did the new church drama group play have a happy ending?'
'Yes! Everyone was delighted when it was over.'

At this moment you are the only man in the C of E who knows what he is doing.
(Seen in the Gents!)

From a Parish Newsletter:
'Children are normally collected during the Offertory Hymn.'

The vicar is away on holiday for
two weeks. Massages can be
given to the curate.

During the absence of our rector,
we enjoyed the rare privilege
of hearing a good sermon
from the bishop.

The sermon next Sunday will be on
hell. A warm welcome will be
extended to all.

The talk for next Friday night will
be 'What is Hell?' Come early and
listen to our choir practice.

The Annual General Meeting in the
Spring, 2000 AD should be hell on
May 10th

This being Easter Sunday, we will ask Mrs Brown, our Sunday School Director, to come forward and lay an egg on the altar.

Thursday at 10 am there will be a meeting of the Little Mothers Club. All those wishing to become little Mothers are welcome to meet our new minister in the manse.

Five

CHURCH OFFICIALS AND COMMITTEES

A sexton is a man who minds his keys and pews.

Dear Jack,
The Vicar here thinks very highly of your father. He's given him a job so important that he has five hundred men under him. He's cutting grass in the churchyard.

Verger, after the sermon to visiting preacher: I did enjoy that passage!
Preacher: Which passage was that, my man?
Verger: Your passage from the pulpit to the vestry!

There is a species of person called a 'Modern Churchman' who draws the full salary of a beneficed clergyman and need not commit himself to any religious belief. *(Evelyn Waugh)*

A vicar's wife was chatting to the churchwarden's wife and confided in her that her husband talked in his sleep. Intrigued, the warden's wife looked forward to sharing this piece of gossip with her husband. She waited till he came home for his evening meal and casually let drop how she had learned that the vicar talked in his sleep.

The warden seemed unimpressed: 'So what!' he said. 'He talks in mine!'

From a speech in the House of Commons:
'Hands off the Church of England, it's the only thing that stands between us and Christianity.'

From a school essay:
'. . . and when the marauders landed on the coast, the villagers would run to the top of the hill and set fire to the deacon . . .'

If you have enough meetings over a long enough period of time, the meetings themselves become more important than the problem they were intended to solve.

A committee is a cul-de-sac into which ideas are lured and then quietly strangled. *(Barnett Cocks)*

A.W. Tozer attended several inconclusive meetings considering some project. After about the sixth meeting Tozer finally rose to leave declaring: 'We've been sitting on this egg long enough and it ain't never going to hatch!'

Nothing is ever accomplished by a committee unless it consists of three members, one of whom happens to be sick and the other absent.

A camel is a horse designed by a committee.

If Moses had been a committee the Israelites would still be in Egypt.

A committee is a group of people who individually can do nothing, but together decide that nothing can be done. *(Fred Allen)*

A committee is a group of the
unwilling, picked from the unfit, to
do the unnecessary.

(Richard Harkness)

Six

THE CONGREGATION

A minister rushed down to the railway station
every single day to watch the 'Ancient
Mariner' chuffing by. There was no chore he
wouldn't interrupt to carry out this ritual.
Members of his congregation were embarrassed by his growing reputation for eccentric-
ity, and asked him to give it up. 'No, broth-
ers,' he said firmly. 'I preach your sermons,
teach your Sunday school, visit the sick, bury
your dead, marry you, and chair every meeting it pleases you to call, but I won't give up
seeing that train go by every day. I'm so
encouraged by it! It's the only thing in the
parish I don't have to push!'

Member: How are you feeling, Pastor?
Pastor: Better.
Member: We had a committee meeting the
other night and they voted to send you this
get-well card. The motion passed 4 to 3!

A minister spoke to a deacon and said, 'I'm told you went to the ball game instead of church this morning.' 'That's completely untrue,' said the deacon, 'and here's the fish to prove it!'

I'm not C. of E. I'm from the Methylated church.

The vicar, looking over the unusually large Easter congregation, announced: 'Dear brethren, I realise that I shall not see many of you again until next Easter, so permit me to take this opportunity to wish you all a very merry Christmas and a most prosperous New Year!'

The parson had announced the first hymn 'Ten thousand time ten thousand!'
Little boy: 'Dad, does he want us to work that one out?'

The doctor went to see her, but the Vicar
    didn't go:
But the doctor had been sent for, and the Vicar
    didn't know.
The doctor got rewarded with a handsome
    little cheque.
But the Vicar for not knowing simply got it in
    the neck.

A parson was officiating at the baptism of the youngest son of a Duke. 'What is the baby's name?' he enquired. 'His name is George Edward David Anthony Carrington-Smyth de Winters Cunningham Digby Cecil Barrington . . .' 'One moment please,' interrupted the parson, 'but could the butler be asked to fetch another bucket of water!'

The seven last words of the church:
'We've never done it that
way before!'

I believe I'm on the 'electrical' roll
of this church.

Seven

CURATES

A curate lost his voice at the local football match one Saturday and, being due to preach the next morning, he thought he should call in and consult his vicar, so he rang the vicarage bell and the door was answered by a very attractive teenage daughter.

'Is the vicar in?' the curate managed to whisper.

'No!' she whispered back thinking she had got the message, 'come in!'

The curate went abroad for his holiday and on return took his unused foreign currency back to the bank to exchange it. Seeing the money the cashier asked him: 'Redemption or conversion, Sir?'

Surprised at the terminology the curate muttered: 'Gosh is this the Bank of England or the Church of England?'

The curate went to the bank and asked for a statement of his account, adding the comment: 'We want to know how far afield we can go for our holiday.' Handing him his statement the cashier enquired of him very gently: 'Have you got a field at the back of your garden, Sir?'

A visiting curate, encouraged by the numbers in church that morning, opened his sermon: 'I have never had the pleasure of preaching to such a dense crowd before.'

Acurate was giving his four-year-old daughter a cuddle before she went to bed. As he picked her up and squeezed her tight, she said, 'Daddy, you're so strong! I really think you'll be God one day!'

There was once a poor curate who was bemoaning his impecunious state in the hearing of his vicar. 'Never mind,' came the rejoinder, 'the fringe benefits are out of this world.'

A curate consistently arrived late for work until his long-suffering vicar asked him what was wrong.
   'My problem,' explained the curate, 'is that I sleep very slowly.'

The vicar of a small village received an invitation to dine one evening with the Squire. As the village was sparsely lit, his Reverence took a lantern to lighten the way through the dark muddy lanes. He had a very enjoyable time and returned home safe and sound. Next morning, he received a note from the Squire: 'Dear Vicar, if you will kindly return the parrot in its cage, you can have your lantern back!'

The new curate was preaching again and, as usual, a lady parishioner who had taken into her head to help train him for his high calling came up with yet another criticism. 'You preached on the sins of the tongue and then you invited all those in the congregation who wanted to dedicate their tongues to come forward at the end of the service and lay them on the altar. That's so ridiculous! How do you think we are all going to put our tongues on that altar?' The curate thought for a moment and turned to the lady: 'You are quite right, sister. Why don't you lay as much as you can on and just let the rest hang over?'

A curate, who had had difficulty holding several positions in parishes, was applying for a new post and the vicar asked him if he was responsible? 'Oh, I'm your man,' said the curate, 'every job I've had, when anything went wrong , they all said I was responsible!'

The BBC issued a storm warning and advised that if anyone had to go out he should wear something white so that he would be clearly visible to motorists. One vicar had to visit a sick parishioner so he decided to put on his surplice over his raincoat. Alas, he was knocked down by a snow plough!

The story is told of a curate who reported to his new boss with a letter from his old vicar which said, 'This man is a great soldier, and he'll be even better if you can cure him of his constant gambling.'

The new boss looked at him sternly and said, 'I hear you're an inveterate gambler. I don't approve. It's bad for discipline and will be a very bad example for the parish. What kind of things do you bet on?'

'Practically anything, sir,' said the curate. 'If you'd like, I'll bet you my next month's pay that you've got a crucifix tattooed under your right shoulder.' The vicar snapped, 'Put down your money.'

He then stripped to the waist, proved conclusively he had no such tattoo, and pocketed the money on the table. He couldn't wait to phone the old vicar and exult, 'That curate of yours won't be in a hurry to make a bet after what I have just done to him.' 'Don't be too sure,' said the old vicar mournfully. 'He just wagered me twenty to two hundred he'd get you to take your shirt off five minutes after he reported for duty!'

He's an original preacher is our new curate. He makes a lot of mistakes but they are different every time.

A conscientious new curate decided to get acquainted with a new family in his congregation and visited them one spring evening. After his knock on the door, a lilting voice from within called out, 'Is that you, Angel?' 'No,' replied the curate, 'but I'm from the same department!'

Poor old Lord Mortlake had only two topics of conversation, his gout and his wife. I never could quite make out which of the two he was talking about. *(Oscar Wilde)*

The curate had stepped in to take the sermon at very short notice, because the vicar was ill. At the end of the sermon he explained apologetically, 'At such short notice I'm afraid I just had to rely on the Holy Spirit. Don't worry, though. It will never happen again.'

A curate in a supermarket was pushing a trolley which contained, among other things, a screaming baby. As he went along the aisles, he kept repeating softly, 'Keep calm, George. Don't get excited George. Don't yell George.'

A lady watched with admiration and then said, 'You are certainly to be commended for your patience in trying to quieten little George.'

'Lady,' the curate declared, '*I'm* George!'

Parishioner's comment about the new curate: 'He lights up a room whenever he leaves it.'

A bore is a man who, when you ask him how he is, tells you.

The most welcome guest is the one who knows when to go home.

The best conversationalist is the person who lets others do the talking.

Every hero becomes a bore at last.
(Ralph Waldo Emerson)

Eight

HOLIDAYS AND HOBBIES

A golfing priest, after having been beaten by an elderly parishioner, returned to the clubhouse somewhat depressed. 'Cheer up,' said the layman. 'Remember, you'll eventually be burying me some day.'

'Yes,', said the priest, 'but even then it will be your hole!' (*Anglican Digest*)

An airliner flew into a violent thunderstorm and was soon bumping around in the sky.

One very nervous lady happened to be sitting next to a clergyman and turned to him for comfort.

'Can't you do something?' she demanded forcefully.

'I'm sorry, ma'am,' said the reverend gently. 'I'm in sales, not management.'

He: Excuse me, stewardess. How high is this plane?
She: About thirty thousand feet.
He: Oh; and how wide is it?

A farmer and his wife went to a fair. The farmer was fascinated by the aeroplane rides, but he balked at the £20 tickets.

'Let's make a deal,' said the pilot. 'If you and your wife can ride without making a single sound, I won't charge you anything. Otherwise you pay the twenty pounds.'

'Good deal!' said the farmer.

So they went for a flight. When they got back the pilot said, 'If I hadn't been there, I would never have believed it. You never made a sound!'

'It wasn't easy, either,' said the farmer. 'I almost yelled when my wife fell out.'

Archaeologist: A man whose
career lies in ruins!

No honest man is a
successful fisherman.

Always choose the oldest customs'
official. No chance of promotion!
(Somerset Maugham)

There is nothing safer than flying –
It's crashing that is dangerous.
(Theo Cowan)

The scientific theory I like best is
that the rings of Saturn are
composed entirely of lost airline
luggage.
(Mark Russell)

An Irish priest on a trip to Israel was horrified when quoted an outrageous price to be ferried across the Sea of Galilee. As he stalked off he was heard muttering, 'No wonder Jesus walked!'

Stewardess: I am sorry, Mr Jones, but we left your wife behind in Chicago.
Man: Thank goodness! I thought I was going deaf!

Bad weather forced a plane to keep on circling over the airfield. Finally, the pilot announced over the P.A. system: 'Ladies and gentlemen, I have some bad news and some good news. The bad news is that we are running out of fuel. The good news is that I am parachuting down to get help.'

A Canadian priest was taking advantage of a cheap holiday in sunny Australia to escape the cold of his home country. He attended the Sunday Eucharist in the cathedral. The Dean noticed him there and asked a sidesman to find out who he was. At the end of the service the sidesman approached the priest and enquired where he was from? 'Saskatoon, Saskatchewan,' replied the priest. The sidesman shook his head and the priest left the cathedral. Later the Dean asked the sidesman if he had found out any details about the visitor: 'Sorry Dean I couldn't. He didn't speak English?'

The vicar sneaked off regularly mid-week for a round of golf instructing his wife to tell the parish he was away on a course. He calmed his conscience by persuading himself that he had a ministry to the handicapped!

O give me the luck to catch a fish
So big that even I
When talking of it afterwards
May have no need to lie.

Customer: Waiter! This coffee tastes like earth! Waiter: I'm not surprised, Sir, it was only ground this morning!

A man with more than a touch of the blarney about him went into a restaurant and said to the waitress, 'A steak, a salad and a kind word.' The waitress went away and a short while later returned with his order.

'What about the kind word?' he asked. She bent over and whispered in his ear, 'Don't eat the steak.'

Man: I can't eat this food! Call
the manager!
Waitress: It's no use, sir. He can't
eat it either.

Some waiters should visit a zoo and
watch the tortoises race by.

Epitaph for a dead waiter – God
finally caught his eye.
(George S. Kaufman)

Remember that by fifty you will
have spent over sixteen years in
bed and three years eating.

'Waiter! Have you got frogs' legs?'
'No Sir, It's just the way I walk.'

Annoyed diner: 'You say you are the same waiter who took my order? Somehow I expected a much older man.'

Nine

HOME AND FAMILY

My son is going through one of those awkward stages, from hooligan to layabout.

Family planning is very important. If I had planned my family it would have been Rockefellers.

The parson, with his family, was on holiday in Europe. He was disturbed to notice his teenage daughter being kissed repeatedly by a French boy.

When she eventually came in he remonstrated and asked her: 'My dear child, why ever didn't you stop him?'

'I couldn't,' she replied, 'I can't speak French!'

Mrs Murphy was speaking to her neighbour: 'Oi don't think my husband has been complately fait'ful to me.'

'Why, Mrs Murphy. What makes you so suspicious?'

'Weel my last child do'nt be lookin' like him one tiny bit!'

Parents' note to son's teacher:
'Please excuse Johnny for being absent, as I was having a baby – and it's not his fault!'

Little boy: 'Mum do we all come from dust?'
'Quite right, son!'
'And do we all return to dust when we die?'
'Yes indeed, son.'
'Well Mum, come and have a look under my bed. There's someone either coming or going!'

The little boy started to cry after a large and friendly dog bounded up to him and licked his hands and face.

'What is the matter?' asked his mother. 'Did he bite you?'

'No,' the child sobbed, 'but he tasted me!'

When asked how she arranged the seating at her dinner parties the hostess replied: 'I never make any special arrangements. Those guests who matter don't mind and those who mind don't matter.'

A young lady had just moved into her new ground floor flat and had invited some friends in to an evening meal for a house warming. The entree was to be lobster and she had it cooked and was dividing it up and placing it in separate dishes when the phone rang. When she came back, to her horror, she found her cat enjoying one of the dishes. She shoo-ed the animal away and replaced the eaten lobster.

In due course her guests arrived and soon it was time to gather at the meal table. Having finished their entree the lady returned to the kitchen to bring on the second course. She happened to glance out of the window and was shocked to see her cat laid out dead on the lawn. The cat had eaten some of that lobster!

She immediately consulted with a doctor on duty at the hospital who said that the only thing for it was to bring everybody round to emergency and have their stomachs pumped!

Highly embarrassed, she returned to her guests and explained the whole story. There could be no delay so they all sped their way to the hospital. None of the guests really wanted to go back for the rest of the meal once their 'pumping' was over and our hostess arrived home very depressed.

Before leaving for work next day, her neighbour tapped on her door to explain that she hadn't liked to disturb her the previous evening as she obviously had guests, but tragically the night before she had been backing her car and ran over her cat!

Mother: What are you doing at the fridge, Willie?
William: Fighting temptation, Mother.

Mealtime is when the youngsters continue eating but sit down.

Eat, drink, and be merry, for
tomorrow ye diet.

Insanity is hereditary; you can get it
from your children.
(*Sam Levenson*)

Advert in newspaper: Home
computer, as new. Never
been figured out.

Having a family is like having
a bowling alley installed in
your head.
(*Martin Mull*)

I have never got over the fact that I
was born in bed with a woman.
(*Wilson Mizner*)

Little Mary, the daughter of a radio announcer who went to church was invited to the vicarage for dinner. The hostess asked if Mary would honour them by saying grace.

Delighted, the little girl cleared her throat, looked at her wrist watch and said, 'This food, friends, is coming to you through the courtesy of Almighty God!'

The little young lady of the house, by way of punishment for some minor misdemeanour, was compelled to eat her dinner alone at a small table in a corner of the dining room. The rest of the family paid no attention to her presence until they heard her audibly praying over her repast with the words, 'Thank you, Lord, for preparing a table before me in the presence of mine enemies.'

Watching your daughter being collected by her date feels like handing over a million dollar Stradivarus to a gorilla. (*Jim Bishop*)

Don't drink nought but water
Was Mum's word to her daughter,
Say 'no' to men,
Be home by ten,
And behave just like you oughta!

Mother: Eat your spinach, dear. It will put colour in your cheeks.
Daughter: Who wants green cheeks.
The old woman had been going on a bit, so when she asked, 'Have I ever told you about my lovely grandchildren?' one of the listeners replied, 'No – and I may say how truly grateful we are that you haven't?'

Any astronomer can predict with absolute accuracy just where every star in the universe will be at 11.30 tonight. He can make no such prediction about his teenage daughter. *(James T. Adams)*

The little boy at the zoo stared at the stork for a long time, then turned to his father and said, 'Gosh, Dad, he doesn't recognise me.'

I know a teenage girl who has been trying to run away from home for a year but every time she gets to the front door the phone rings.

Home wasn't built in a day.

Ten

LEADERSHIP

A leader is one who knows the way, goes the way and shows the way.

(John Maxwell)

1) When in charge, ponder.
2) When in trouble, delegate.
3) When in doubt, mumble. *(James Boren)*

In some countries a government leader can't be sure whether the people are following him or chasing him.

The church has been subnormal for so long that when it becomes normal it is judged abnormal.

Diplomacy: The art of saying things in such a way that nobody knows exactly what you mean.

Leadership: The world spins around so fast that no one sits on the top of it for very long.

Experience: Yesterday's answers to today's problems.

Business: Never mistake motion for action.
(Ernest Hemingway)

Decisiveness: The decision is 'maybe' and that's final.

Last Resort: When all else fails, read the instructions.

A leader is a dealer in hope.

A common liturgy in song
unites us.

Eleven

MISSIONARIES

Missionaries are told they need
a strong sense of humour and a
weak sense of smell.

'I don't like the look of the new missionary,'
said one cannibal to the other. 'That's all right,'
said the other, 'just eat the vegetables.'

The only thing that keeps our mission house
from falling down is that the termites are holding hands.

First pioneer missionary: Why are you wearing
only one spur?
Second pioneer missionary: Well, I figure
when one side of the horse starts running, the
other side will too.

Did you hear about the cannibal who had chronic indigestion? He kept on eating people who disagreed with him.

A cannibal, feeling a bit peckish, gobbled up a Methodist missionary for his elevenses. He then ate a Catholic priest for lunch and an Anglican bishop for supper. That night he couldn't sleep with a terrible pain in his stomach which still distressed him in the morning, so he was obliged to call for the witchdoctor. The witchdoctor examined him and when he heard what he had been eating recently he knew what the problem was and gave the cannibal his diagnosis. 'You are experiencing an ecumenical movement!'

When the missionaries came to Africa they had the Bible and we had the land. They said, 'Let us pray.' We closed our eyes. When we opened them we had the Bible and they had the land. (Desmond Tutu)

A missionary in Chile was learning to ride a horse, an animal with which he was totally unfamiliar. 'I don't like the look of its head,' he complained to his riding instructor. 'Don't worry,' replied the instructor, 'you'll soon get over that!'

Observing a missionary on his
mountain bike, one cannibal turned
to the other and said,
'Oh good! Meals on wheels!'

One cannibal turned to another.
'Let's go down to the campfire
and see who's cooking.'

Twelve

MONEY AND GIVING

Hoping to develop his son's character, a father once gave him a fifty pence piece and a ten pence piece as he was leaving for Sunday school. 'Now, Bill, you put whichever one you want on the offering plate,' he said.

When the boy returned, his father asked which coin he had given. Bill answered, 'Well, just before they sent around the plate the preacher said, "The Lord loveth a cheerful giver," and I knew I could give the ten pence a lot more cheerfully than I could give the fifty pence, so I gave it.'

Parishioner: 'I have nothing but praise for the new vicar.'
Sidesman: 'I noticed that when I came round with the plate last Sunday.'

Vicar's announcement: I've always said that the poor were welcome in this church and I see by the offerings that they are coming!

To get his wealth he spent his health
And then with might and main
He turned around and spent his wealth
To get his health again.

Then there was the Irish kidnapper who
enclosed a stamped addressed envelope with
the ransom demand.

Parish Stewardship:
Take my silver and my gold.
Not a mite would I withhold.
But as times are rather hard,
Please accept my Barclaycard.

Henry Ford, on a visit to Dublin, offered a donation of £1,000 towards the building of a new hospital in the city. The *Dublin Times* accidentally on purpose announced that he had promised £10,000 and praised his wonderful generosity. It was pointed out that it would look very bad if a correction had to be printed and consequently Henry Ford agreed to the larger amount. He did, however, make a condition. When the new hospital was ready, it should have an appropriate Bible text framed and hung in the entrance hall. His text was Matthew 25 v 35: 'I was a stranger and ye took me in.'

In the midst of life we are in debt.

(Ethel Mumford)

Nowadays we spend so much
on luxuries we can't afford
the necessities.

Thirteen

POPES AND PRELATES

The Pope was once asked how many people work in the Vatican and he replied: 'About 50 per cent.'

The Pope was asking the Lord certain questions of major concern to the Church:
Pope: Lord will the Church ever allow priests to marry?
God: Not in your lifetime.
Pope: And, Lord, will the Church ever have women priests?
God: Not in your lifetime.
Pope: One final question, Lord? Will there be another Polish Pope?
After a long pause, God replied: 'Not in My lifetime?'

A drunk boards the train and sits himself down beside a priest and begins to read the paper.
After a bit he looks up and says: 'Tell me Father, what causes arthritis?'

This was just the opening the priest was waiting for. 'I will tell you what causes arthritis, my man,' he said with some passion. 'It's immoral living, too much drinking and smoking and other sins of the flesh. How long have you had it?'

'Oh it's not me, Father,' said the drunk. 'It says here that the Pope's got it!'

It often happens that I wake at night and begin to think about a serious problem and decide I must tell the Pope about it. Then I wake up completely and remember that I am the Pope. *(Pope John XXIII)*

My love life is so bad I'm taking part in the world celibacy championships. I meet the Pope in the semi-finals. *(Guy Bellamy)*

It is said that Prime Minister Disraeli once consulted with Queen Victoria against the appointment of Bishop Tait as Archbishop of Canterbury: 'There is in his idiosyncrasy a strange fund of enthusiasm, a quality which ought never to be possessed by an Archbishop of Canterbury or a Prime Minister of England.'

A little girl told her mother: 'We went to a confirmation service at the cathedral and I saw the bishop. Now I know what a crook looks like!'

A clergyman complained to his bishop about
the nasty habit of name-dropping that was
beginning to become commonplace in the diocese. 'Quite right!' responded the bishop, 'the
Queen and I are very concerned about it!'

A mother carefully instructed her little daughter about the correct way to address an archbishop. When you speak to him, she said, you
must always say 'Your Grace'. The little girl
approached William Temple bowed her head
and said sweetly, 'For what we are about to
receive may the Lord make us truly thankful!'

The late Archbishop Temple, when he was pri-
mate of England, related this story. One morning, in a house where he was a guest, he heard
from the kitchen a voice singing lustily,
'Nearer My God to Thee'. He reflected on the
piety of the woman who went about her morning tasks to the strains of the noble hymn, and
so spoke of it to his host.

'Oh, yes,' replied the host. 'That's the
hymn she boils the eggs to – three verses for
soft boil and five for hard.'

An archbishop was seated next to a duchess at
dinner when he suddenly went pale and
uttered a doleful groan. 'Can we help, your
Grace?' asked the duchess in concern.

'I have always feared I might lose the feeling in my leg as my old father did,' said the archbishop, 'and now I can't feel a thing in my left thigh – I have just been pinching it and there's no feeling there at all'.

'Your Grace, if its any consolation,' said the duchess, 'its my right thigh you have been clutching for the last five minutes!'

A vicar and his wife from the country were invited to stay at Lambeth Palace and were nervous about proper table manners in such company. They decided they would never make a first move and just copy everything at meal times that the Archbishop did. All went well the first night but at breakfast the next morning when they saw the Archbishop pour milk into his saucer they did the same. The Archbishop added some cream and sugar and they followed suit. Finally the Archbishop bent down and placed his saucer on the floor for the palace cat!

An archbishop of Canterbury was a distinguished guest at a mayoral dinner. As the first course was being served a waiter accidentally dropped a whole bowl of hot soup into his Grace's lap. The archbishop looked around the table despairingly and said: 'Is there any layman present who will be good enough to express my feelings?'

A Victorian archbishop, taking his last Confirmation, placed his episcopal hands on the head of a bald man and found himself declaring absent-mindedly, 'I declare this stone well and truly laid!'

Archbishop Donald Coggan had just gone to Bradford, his first diocese. Coming out of a conference he was greeted by a very excited little man. 'Oh, bishop, this is the first opportunity I have had to shake your hand. I'm so glad! I'm sure that under your guidance in this diocese things will go from bad to worse!'

Archbishop Michael Ramsey was a one-time canon of Durham. The dean's wife wrote to a friend: 'He is nice. But he has no small talk. He can only talk about the Atonement. But unfortunately or not, that is not the subject which is usually in our minds.'

Friends at Durham recollected with some amusement the clumsy way that Michael Ramsey was learning to ride a bicycle when he was there, but the truth was that whenever Ramsey rode a bicycle he looked as though he was learning to ride.

The Queen was showing the Archbishop around the Royal Stables when one of the stallions broke wind so loudly that it could not be ignored. 'Oh dear!' said the Queen, 'How embarrassing! I am so sorry about that!'

'Its quite understandable,' said the Archbishop, and after a moment of thought, he added: 'As a matter of fact, I thought it was the horse.'

Geoffrey Fisher was making his first visit to the United States aboard the *Queen Elizabeth* as Archbishop of Canterbury. As soon as the ship docked, a swarm of reporters arrived to interview him. He prided himself on his ability to parry awkward questions. Within seconds, one was flung at him: 'Archbishop, do you intend to visit the night clubs in New York?' With a wry smile, the Archbishop countered, 'Why, are there any night clubs in New York?' His self-congratulation lasted only until the morning papers arrived. A banner headline said, 'ARCHBISHOP'S FIRST QUESTION: ARE THERE ANY NIGHT CLUBS IN NEW YORK?'

Fourteen

PRAYERS AND GRACES

'Pray for my soul! More things are wrought by prayer than this world dreams of.' *(Tennyson)*

A minister, at the end of a week of missionary activity in the church prayed fervently: 'And any spark of grace that has been kindled by these exercises, O, Lord, we pray Thee, water that spark!'

A Presbyterian minister, called at short notice to officiate at the parish church of Crathie in the presence of Queen Victoria, was so overpowered by the magnificence of the occasion that he broke out into a mighty prayer:

'Grant that as she grows to be an old woman, she may be made a new man; and that in all righteous causes she may go forth before her people like a he-goat on the mountains!'

A newly elected MP saw a fellow MP on his knees and asked him: 'Are you praying for the House?'

'No!' replied the other MP, 'I've seen the House and I am now praying for the country!'

Little girl after her geography exam: 'Please God make Copenhagen the capital of Japan for a month.'

A little girl was praying for her lately deceased grandmother during a period of very cold weather. 'Dear God, please bless Mummy and Daddy and make it hot for Granny.'

Instead of ending the public prayer with the words 'world without end, Amen', a young curate became nervous and tongue-tied and concluded with the words 'God without end. Amen'.

Another curate invited the congregation to confess their sins to God in the words of the 'General Thanksgiving'.

Little William was saying his prayers one night. His mother tiptoed up and heard him say, 'And please make Tommy stop throwing things at me. You may remember, I've mentioned this before. He's still doing it.'

Little boy's prayers: 'Dear God – same as last night – Amen.'

A Sunday school teacher asked a little girl if she said her prayers every night.
'No, not every night,' declared the child.
' 'Cause some nights I don't want anything!'

Little Susie concluded her prayer by saying: 'Dear God, before I finish, please take care of Daddy, take care of Mummy, take care of my baby brother, Grandma and Grandpa . . . and please, God, take care of yourself, or else we're all sunk!'

Johnny, praying in a loud voice before his birthday:
'Dear God, I pray that I will get a new bicycle for my birthday.'
His brother: 'What are you shouting for? God isn't deaf.'
Johnny: 'I know, I know, but Granny is.'

Little Jimmy had finished his nightly prayer and asked me what prayers were. I told him they were little messages to God. Quickly he said, 'Oh, yes! And we send them at night to get the cheaper rates.'

A young midshipman asked Nelson, on the
eve of the Battle of Trafalgar, if he could offer
up a prayer to God. 'Of course you can, my
dear boy,' replied Nelson. The midshipman
knelt on the deck and looked up to heaven:

'Lord,' he said, 'I know that if it's your will,
tomorrow we'll win this great battle. I also
realise that if it's your will, the French will win.
If you could possibly stay out of it altogether
though, we'll thrash the blighters anyway.'

A priest went to see O'Reilly in hospital. 'I'm
going to pray,' he said, 'that you'll forgive
McCann for hitting you with that bottle.'

'There's no need to waste your time, Father.
Wait till I get better, and then pray for
McCann.'

An elderly vicar once prayed for
that world which the peace
cannot give.

Fifteen

PULPITS, PREACHERS AND TEACHERS

I'm going to read this sermon.
Unlike my fellow clergy I like to
know where I am going!

A rector once arranged for his curate to prepare six suitable addresses for Lent. The curate gave the first address and went on for ages. When they entered the vestry after the service the rector put one hand on the curate's shoulder and clapping his other hand to his own forehead he declaimed: 'Oh whatever shall we do? When I asked you to prepare six addresses I did not mean you to give them all at one go!'

A priest accidentally tore his cassock ascending the pulpit, making a loud ripping sound. To make matters worse he announced his text: 'Rend your hearts and not your garments!'

An American bishop once addressed the subject of preaching with his clergy and gave them a hint: 'If you don't strike oil in ten minutes stop boring!'

In introducing this subject I feel like a mosquito in a nudist camp – I hardly know where to begin!

I wouldn't say he's imitative. Then again he's the only man I know who has a hernia from lifting ideas.

A journey of a thousand miles begins with trying to find a place to park your car near the church!

A genius is a man who can rewrap a new shirt and not have any pins left over.

(Dino Levi)

Good evening, ladies and gentlemen. You'll be glad to know that when I asked my secretary to type this sermon out for me I asked her to eliminate any thing that was dull or confusing. So in conclusion . . .

I have an eighty-year-old grandmother who feels perfectly safe thanks to three things – a vodofone, a bullet-proof vest and the 1662 Book of Common Prayer.

An old lady went to church and heard the young curate preach. When she was leaving someone asked her what she thought of him. 'Well,' she said, 'he was truly apostolic. He took a text and went everywhere preaching the gospel.'

For the last three weeks I have been practising this sermon in front of my dog so if you want to make me feel at home when I've finished, don't clap – just bark!

Priest: Are you a soldier in the army of the Lord?
Man: Yes Father!
Priest: Then how come we only see you at Christmas and Easter?
Man: I'm in the Secret Service, Father.

Three Scandinavian priests were sentenced to death and were given one last wish.

The Dane asked if he could have a plate full of Danish pastries.

The Swede asked if he could preach just one more sermon.

The Norwegian just begged to be shot before the Swede started preaching!

The priest had spent a lot of time preparing his sermon and was disappointed to find a congregation of one elderly farmer.

He enquired if he would like to hear the sermon. 'If I took a bucket to the yard and only one hen turned up, I'd still feed her,' said the farmer; so the priest delivered his hour-long address.

Afterwards the farmer added a further comment: 'I said I'd feed her but I'm blowed if I'd give her the whole bucketful. (*Lisa Brimson in the* Church Times)

The parson had mentioned all the books in the Old Testament and finally came to Malachi: 'Ah Malachi,' he droned on, 'where shall we put Malachi?'

Suddenly a voice from the back piped up: 'He can come and sit here – I'm going.'

A humble Chilean was giving his mule its midday feed and attaching a nose bag to the animal's head so that it could munch its lunch at leisure. He had nearly finished when a *roto* (tramp), rather the worse for drink, staggered across the road shaking his head and shouting: 'You'll never do it, you'll never do it.'

The mule's owner was puzzled: 'Never do what?' he asked.

'You'll never get that great big animal into that tiny little bag,' he said. This is surely the predicament of a preacher limited by so little time to deliver his soul!

A Cornish open-air preacher was holding forth outside an English pub inveigling against the ills of drink.
Voice from the crowd: 'I thought yer said we was to love our enemies.'
Cornish preacher: 'Yer'e quite right. I did!'
Voice: 'Well I love whisky – that's my enemy.'
(Laughter all round)
Cornish preacher: 'But since when did I tell yer to swaller yer enemies?'

A man got up in the middle of the vicar's sermon and walked out. His very embarrassed wife approached the vicar afterwards to apologise. 'I hope you didn't think vicar that he disagreed with anything you said. He just has a tendency to walk in his sleep.'

We welcome our preacher this morning. Every sermon he preaches is better than the next one.

Billy Graham once had to preach in the Roker Park stadium in Sunderland (26/5/84). He said it was the coldest day he'd ever preached in the open-air. He wore a cloth cap, two sweaters, two sets of thermal underwear, two pairs of thermal socks. A wag commented later that he must have preached St Long-John's Gospel.

Dr Alexander Findlay was a notable New Testament scholar and a Methodist preacher. He was also a very humble man and his slightly faded appearance belied his great scholarship and gifts as a preacher.

On one Sunday he went to preach at a morning service where the main church door was reached up a steep flight of stone steps. At the bottom he encountered an elderly lady who was looking rather nervously at the climb which faced her. With characteristic courtesy Dr Findlay proffered his arm and together they ascended the steps. On reaching the door the old lady turned to her kind escort and asked: 'You wouldn't happen to know who is preaching this morning, would you?' 'Dr Alexander Findlay!' came the reply. 'Oh,' said the old lady, 'then would you mind helping me down the steps again?' And he did.

In some countries people are put
to death by elocution.

Three rules for successful speakers
– stand up, speak up, shut up.

Remember the longer the spoke
the greater the tyre.

I can eat alphabet soup and
preach better sermons!

What do I think of Western civilisa-
tion? I think it would be a very
good idea. *(Mahatma Gandhi)*

A mistake is at least evidence that
someone tried to do something.

A man stayed at home while his wife went to church. When she returned, he enquired about the sermon. She said it was OK.

'Well what did the vicar preach about?' the man persisted.

'I don't know,' said his wife, 'he never did say!'

The vicar appeared in the pulpit one Sunday with a generous piece of sticky plaster on his face: 'I was concentrating on my sermon this morning when shaving and I cut myself.'

After the service a church member approached him: 'That's too bad about your accident! Better concentrate on your shaving and cut your sermon next time!'

The Reverend Henry Ward Beecher entered Plymouth Church on Sunday and found several letters awaiting him. One of them contained the single word, 'Fool'. Quietly he decided to bring this to the attention of the congregation and announced:

'I have known many an instance of a man writing a letter and forgetting to sign his name, but this is the only instance I have ever known of a man signing his name and forgetting to write the letter.'

Wrote a rector to his parishioner: 'Do you think I should put more fire into my sermons?' 'No, just the opposite,' came the reply.

Little girl to mummy: 'Mummy, why does the pastor pray before he goes up into the pulpit?'

She replied, 'He's asking God to help him preach a good sermon.'

Little girl: 'Then why doesn't God answer his prayer?'

A minister asked a little girl what she thought of her first church service.

'The music was nice,' she said, 'but the commercial was too long.'

A Free Church advertised for a new pastor who was able to walk on water and move mountains. The man who got the job turned up for his interview with a life jacket and a pick-axe.

One Sunday a vicar was waxing eloquent about how he could see a sermon in every blade of grass.

The next day a country yokel was cycling past the vicarage and spotted the incumbent mowing his lawn. 'That's roight, Vicar, that's roight! Keep 'em short. Keep 'em short!'

At the end of the service a woman thanked the pastor for his sermon. 'I found it so helpful,' she told him. The minister responded, 'I hope it will not prove so helpful as the last sermon you heard me preach.' The puzzled woman asked, 'Why, what do you mean?' 'Well,' explained the clergyman, 'that sermon lasted you three months!'

The minister was visiting an old lady who was dying. She told him she could not wait for the angels to come and carry her to Isaac's bosom.

The minister who well knew the biblical passage she was referring to corrected her quietly; 'You mean Abraham's bosom my dear!'

'Parson,' she said, 'when you have been on the shelf as long as I have you don't really mind whose bosom it is!'

Going out of church one Sunday morning, a Lancashire man was greeted by his friend Joe, who had been waiting twenty minutes for him.

'Tha's late,' said Joe.

'Aye.'

'Parson bin a bit long-winded?'

'Aye.'

' 'appen he hasn't finished yet?'

'Oh, aye, he finished a long while sin' but he won't stop.'

More than any time in history mankind faces a crossroads. One path leads to despair and utter hopelessness, the other to total destruction. Let us pray that we have the wisdom to choose correctly. *(Woody Allen)*

A clergyman was visiting to officiate in a remote country church. He was greatly scandalised to see the verger lift a silver half-crown coin from the offertory plate and put it into his own pocket before he presented the collection at the rails for blessing. After the service he felt obliged to challenge the verger and told him with emotion that his evil crime had been discovered. The verger looked puzzled for a moment and then a sudden light dawned on him, 'Woy Sir, you don't mean that old half crown o'mine? Woy oive "led off" with that thar coin for the last thirty years.'

There was an old clergyman so besotted with cricket that he occasionally said 'Over' instead of 'Amen'. On one celebrated occasion he walked from the lectern having proclaimed, 'Here endeth the second innings.' When he had a parish hall built, he had signs for the doors, one which said 'Out', and the other 'Not out'. He even liked to preach on the game and his favourite texts were: 'Peter stood up with the eleven and was bold' (*Acts 2:14*), 'I caught you by guile' (*2 Cor 12:16*), '. . . drinking in the pavilions' (*I Kings 20:12*) etc.

The Vicar announced one Sunday that he was leaving the parish to take up another post elsewhere in the Diocese. He was quite touched afterwards to find the old verger sitting at the back of the church with his head in his hands and his eyes full of tears. He tried to reassure him. 'Don't get upset,' he said, 'there will soon be another Vicar here and I've no doubt he will be a lot better than me.' 'Oh no, he won't,' said the old man, 'the last Vicar said the same thing when he went and it wasn't true.'

I resigned because of illness and fatigue. The congregation were sick and tired of me. (*A. Vicar*)

The secret of a good sermon is to have a good beginning and a good ending and having the two as close together as possible.
(George Burns)

America has become so tense and nervous, it's been years since I've seen anyone asleep in church.
(Norman Vincent Peale)

A good sermon should be like a woman's skirt; short enough to rouse interest, but long enough to cover the essentials.
(Ronald Knox)

Few sinners are saved after the first twenty minutes of a sermon.
(Mark Twain)

Clerical retirement doesn't reduce
us all to cleriatrics!

What he lacked in depth as a
preacher he made up for in length.
(Mark Twain)

The sermon was a great success,
but the congregation was a disaster.

Get your facts right first and then
you can distort them as much as
you please.
(Mark Twain)

If all the people who went to sleep
during sermons were laid out on
the ground end to end they would
be a lot more comfortable.

Bored with the sermon, a little boy suddenly spied an engraved list of names on the wall of all the men from the parish who had died in the Services. Not able to contain his worry any longer the little boy nudged his father and pointed to the plaque asking with some urgency: 'Which service, Dad, morning or evening?'

The sermon was very long this Sunday morning and little Danny was getting more restless by the minute. Suddenly, in a whisper too loud for his mother's comfort, he blurted out, 'If we give him the money now, Mum, will he let us go out?'

A vicar about to retire was explaining his difficulty: 'For the last ten years I have been running this parish on amnesia but this last year I have even run out of amnesia.'

An Irish garda (policeman) stopped a priest in his car. 'Would you be having a driver's licence, Father?' he asked.
'Indeed I have,' said the priest.
'Well that's good because if you didn't I'd have to see it.'

The vicar took his rather old car to the garage for an oil change. After the mechanic had briefly inspected under the bonnet he turned to the vicar: 'If I were you vicar I'd keep the oil and change the car!'

If you are unhappy with your vicar, simply have your church wardens send off a copy of this letter to six other churches who are tired of their vicar. Then bundle up your vicar and send him to the church at the top of the list of this letter. Within a week you will receive 16,435 vicars and one of them should be all right. Have faith in this chain letter for vicars. Do not break the chain. One church did and got their old vicar back again!

The parish priest was always a welcome visitor for short-sighted Mrs O'Hara. 'But that wasn't the priest,' exclaimed her daughter, after the man had just left, 'that was the doctor.'
'Oh was it indeed to goodness,' she replied with relief, 'I t'ought our priest was getting a bit too familiar.'

Then there was the Irish priest who went to buy a new dip stick because his old one wouldn't reach the oil.

There is not the least use in preaching to anyone unless you chance to catch them ill.

(Sydney Smith)

Our Vicar left three months ago so we gave him a little momentum from the parish.

If 'tongues' gives you a headache then Toronto will give you a heart attack!

The centre of church life lies on its circumference

The church that lives to itself will die to itself.

(Michael Ramsey)

Theological Education

A lecture is a process by which the notes of the professor become the notes of the students without passing through the minds of either.
(R.K. Rathbun)

I know you believe you understand what you think I said. But I am not sure you realise that what you heard is not what I meant.
(Patrick Murray)

Peeved lecturer (who had told a story that failed to produce the expected outburst): 'Well, I suppose you lot will laugh at that story next summer.'

Voice from back of lecture hall: 'No, sir; we laughed at it last summer.'

Jesus said to them: 'Who do you say that I am?'

They replied. 'You are the eschatological manifestation of the ground of our being, the *kerygma* of which we find the ultimate meaning of our interpersonal relationships.'

And Jesus said: 'What?'

Q. What is the difference between God and Professor . . . ?
A. God is here but everywhere. Professor . . . is everywhere but here.

Sixteen

RELIGION AND GOD

Some people use religion like a bus – they ride on it only while it is going their way.

A man fell off a cliff but managed to grab hold of a branch on his way down. He hung there and shouted to the top, 'Is anybody up there?'
'Yes,' came the reply, 'God is up here!'
'Can you help me, God?'
'Yes.'
'What do you want me to do?'
'Let go of the branch.'
There was an agonising pause.
'Is there anybody else up there?'

The world is equally shocked at hearing Christianity criticised and seeing it practised.
(D. Elton Trueblood)

'Mum, does God use our bathroom?'
'No, why on earth should he do that?'
'Because Dad was standing outside the door this morning muttering "My God, are you still in there?" '

Teacher: 'Stand up all the children who want to go to heaven.'
They all stood up except Jack.
'Don't you want to go to heaven, Jack?'
'Not yet, Miss,' said Jack.

Tradition is the living faith of the dead. Honour it! Traditionalism is the dead faith of the living. Abandon it!

One day during the French Revolution, a man remarked to Talleyrand, who was also a Bishop: 'The Christian religion – what is it? It would be easy to start a religion like that.'
'Oh, yes,' replied Talleyrand. 'One would only have to get crucified and rise again on the third day.' *(Baptist Review)*

Praise expresses the marvel of not being the centre of the universe ourselves. *(Cardinal Carlo-Maria Martini)*

Nowadays the only time a person
gets on his knees is to look for his
contact lenses.

As God once said, and I think quite
rightly . . .
(Margaret Thatcher)

Southern California is known for its
avant-God religions.

Graffiti: Is reincarnation making
a comeback?

The lion and the lamb shall lie
down together, but the lamb
won't get much sleep.

Why do born-again people so often make you wish they had never been born the first time? *(Katherine Whitehorn)*

Things have come to a pretty pass when religion is allowed to invade the sphere of private life. *(W.L. Melbourne)*

I was raised in the Jewish tradition, taught never to marry a Gentile woman, shave on a Saturday night and, most especially, never to shave a Gentile woman on a Saturday night. *(Woody Allen)*

Jesus was born on a bank holiday and died on a bank holiday. We can therefore assume that when he returns again it will also be on a bank holiday. *(P.G. Johnson)*

He was of the faith chiefly in the sense that the church he currently did not attend was Catholic. *(Kingsley Amis)*

A clergyman, visiting the zoo, was very excited to see a lion and a lamb lying down together in the same cage. The vicar went to congratulate the zoo-keeper saying that it was quite amazing to be witnessing the fulfilment of the Church's peaceful vision for the mille-nium. Whereupon the appreciative keeper whispered confidentially into the vicar's ear:

'Vicar, I must let you into a little secret; that there lamb 'ave to be replaced pretty often!'

Seventeen

VIRTUES AND VICES

Happiness is a place between too little and too much.

Abraham Lincoln was questioned by one of his advisers as follows: 'Mr President, I cannot understand you. You treat your enemies with such kindness. It would seem to me that you should want to destroy them.'

'My dear fellow,' said the President, 'I do destroy my enemy when I make him into a friend.'

'I have often had to eat my words and I must confess that I have found it a wholesome diet.' *(Winston Churchill)*

Nothing is more simple than greatness; indeed, to be simple is to be great. *(Ralph Waldo Emerson)*

You can make more friends in two months by becoming interested in other people than you can in two years by trying to get other people interested in you. *(Dale Carnegie)*

Kindness is the ·inability to remain at ease in the presence of another person who is ill at ease, the inability to remain comfortable in the presence of another who is uncomfortable, the inability to have peace of mind when one's neighbour is troubled. *(Rabbi Samuel H. Holdenson)*

Gratitude is the most exquisite form of courtesy.

Thrift is the most admirable virtue of any ancestor!

'My boy,' a father advised his son, 'treat everybody with politeness, even those who are rude to you. For remember that you show courtesy to others not because they are gentlemen, but because you are one.'

There is only one immutable law in life – in a gentleman's toilet, incoming traffic has the right of way. *(Hugh Leonard)*

He: My wife just got a ticket for speeding.
Him: That's nothing! My wife is so bad the
       police gave her a season ticket.

The stalled car sat dead still at the traffic lights
as they went from red, to green, to amber, to
red, to green, to amber, to red. Finally, a
policeman came up and said, 'Pardon me, sir,
but don't we have any colour that you like?'

A policeman stopped a man driving the wrong
way on a one-way street. 'Didn't you see the
arrow?' he demanded.
    'Arrow? Honest, officer, I didn't even see
the Indians.'

Sheriff apologetically: 'Excuse me for being
nervous,' he said, as he slipped the noose over
the condemned man's head. 'This is my first
hanging.'
Prisoner: 'Mine too!'

There are three types of people: those who
make things happen; those who watch things
happen, and those who haven't a clue what's
happening!

A scorpion, being a poor swimmer, asked a turtle to carry him on his back across the river.

'Are you mad?' exclaimed the turtle. 'You'll sting me while I'm swimming and I'll drown!'

'My dear turtle,' laughed the scorpion, 'if I were to sting you, you would drown and I would go down with you! Now where is the logic in that?'

'You're right!' cried the turtle. 'Hop on!'

The scorpion climbed aboard and, halfway across the river, gave the turtle a nasty sting. As they both sank to the bottom, the turtle asked resignedly, 'Do you mind if I ask you something? You said there'd be no logic in your stinging me. Why did you do it?'

'It had nothing to do with logic,' the drowning scorpion replied, sadly, 'It's just my character.'

> Procrastination is my sin,
> It brings me naught but sorrow.
> I know that I should stop it,
> In fact, I will – tomorrow!
> (Gloria Pitzer)

Sleep with clean hands, either kept clean all day by integrity or washed clean at night by repentance. (John Donne)

Some people are easily entertained.
All you have to do is sit down and
listen to them.

'Lord, give me chastity. But not yet!'
(the young St Augustine)

You can never do a kindness too
soon because you never know how
soon it may be too late.

Always borrow money from a
pessimist. He doesn't expect
to get it back.

He is no fool who gives up what he
cannot keep to gain what he can
never lose.
(Jim Elliot)

A father repeatedly told his little boy to sit down on the back seat of the car. He remained standing, however, until eventually, exasperated, the father physically sat the boy down.

The little boy grimaced and muttered, 'I may be sitting down on the outside, but I'm still standing up on the inside!'

A man wrote to the Inland Revenue: 'I can't sleep at night, so I'm enclosing £100 I forgot to declare.
PS: If I still can't sleep, I will send the rest.'

The church treasurer was giving his report at the Annual General Parochial Council. He reminded them that last year 'we were on the edge of precipice but this year we have made a big leap forward'.

'Hey, do you remember when I was broke the last time you helped me out and I said I would never forget you?'
  'Yes.'
  'Well I haven't forgotten and I'm broke again!'

Men occasionally stumble over the truth, but most of them pick themselves up and hurry off as if nothing had happened. *(Winston Churchill)*

Several years ago the *British Weekly* printed a letter to the editor:

'Dear Sir,
I notice that ministers seem to set a great deal of importance on their sermons and spend a great deal of time in preparing them. I have been attending services quite regularly for the past thirty years and have listened to no less than three thousand sermons. But, to my consternation, I discover I cannot remember a single one of them. I wonder if a minister's time might be more profitably spent on something else?
Yours sincerely . . .

That letter triggered off an avalanche of angry responses. Sermons were castigated and defended by lay people and clergy, but eventually a single letter closed the debate:

'Dear Sir,
I have been married for thirty years. During that time I have eaten 32,000 meals – mostly of my wife's cooking. Suddenly, I have discovered that I cannot remember the menu of a single meal. And yet, I received nourishment from every one of them. I have the distinct impression that without them I would have starved to death long ago.
Yours sincerely . . . *(James Berkley)*

All the holy men seem to have gone off and died. There's no one left but us sinners to carry on the ministry. *(Jamie Buckingham)*

Three boy scouts told the Scoutmaster they had done a really 'good deed' for that day.

'Well boys, what did you do?' asked the Scoutmaster.

'We helped an old lady across the street,' the boys chimed in unison.

'And did it take all three of you to do that?' asked the Scoutmaster suspiciously.

'Yes it did,' chorused the boys. Then the smallest one added, 'She didn't want to go!'

After checking the licence of the driver he'd stopped, the highway patrolman said, 'It says here you're supposed to be wearing glasses.'

'But officer, I have contacts.'

'I don't care who you know, you're breaking the law.'

Patience: The willingness to listen to the other person tell you their troubles before you tell them yours.

Patience: The ability to listen silently while someone else tells all about the very operation you just underwent.

Happiness is having a scratch for
every itch.
(Ogden Nash)

Happiness is the interval between
periods of unhappiness.

What's the use of *happiness*? It can't
buy you money.
(Henry Youngman)

I can resist everything except
temptation.
(Oscar Wilde)

When women kiss, it always
reminds me of prize-fighters
shaking hands.
(H.L. Mencken)

Closer to the truth than he meant to be was the schoolboy who wrote on an examination paper: 'The Armistice was signed on the eleventh of November in 1918, and since then once in every year there has been two minutes of peace.'

The word *good* has many meanings. For example, if a man were to shoot his grandmother at a range of five hundred yards, I should call him a good shot, but not necessarily a good man. *(G.K. Chesterton)*

First left, go along the corridor. You'll see a door marked Gentlemen, but don't let that deter you. *(F.E. Smith)*

Giving up smoking is the easiest thing in the world. I know because I've done it thousands of times. *(Mark Twain)*

The English country gentleman galloping after a fox – the unspeakable in full pursuit of the uneatable. *(Oscar Wilde)*

It is going to be fun to watch and see how long the meek can keep the earth after they inherit it. *(Kin Hubbard)*

'Criticism . . . is like pain in the human body. It is not pleasant but where would the body be without it?' *(Winston Churchill)*

'When preaching of heaven, let your face light up with the glory of it. When preaching of hell, your ordinary face will do!' *(Charles H. Spurgeon on preaching)*

'If I had to face only the Sermon on the Mount, and my own interpretation of it, I should not hesitate to say "Oh yes, I am a Christian" . . . 'But negatively I can tell you that much of what passes as Christianity is a negation of the Sermon on the Mount. And please mark my words. I am not at the present moment speaking of Christian conduct. I am speaking of Christian belief. Of Christianity as it is known in the West.' *(Mahatma Ghandi)*

A diplomat is a person who can tell you to go to hell in such a way that you actually look forward to the trip. *(Caskie Stinnet)*

Always remember the poor – it costs nothing.

(Josh Billings)

Etiquette is knowing how to yawn
with your mouth closed.

In England nobody goes to the
theatre unless he or she has
bronchitis.
(James Agate)

'We shall all be judged by history
and I'm going to write the history.'
(Winston Churchill)

Don't just do something:
stand there!

'Sometimes there is wisdom in
letting things slide for a while.'
(Winston Churchill)

'Laugh a little and teach your men to laugh
. . . If you can't smile, grin. If you can't grin
keep out of the way until you can.' *(Winston
Churchill)*

'Every night I try myself by Court Marshall to
see if I have done anything effective during the
day.' *(Winston Churchill)*

'There is never a good time to take
a holiday so take one anyway.'

(Winston Churchill)

Eighteen

VICARS

Old Jack had been a faithful Christian and was in hospital thought to be near death. The vicar went to visit him. Standing over him by the bedside to pray for him he observed his condition deteriorating rapidly and the sick man motioned frantically for something to write on. The vicar found pen and paper and old Jack had no sooner scribbled his note than he fell back dead. With all the rush of nurses and doctors the vicar forgot about the note which he pocketed.

At the funeral, he was finishing his address when he suddenly remembered the note still in his pocket and so he thought it might add some interest to the solemn occasion if he read it out to everyone.

'Jack gave me a note just before he died and I think this would be a lovely time to share it,' said the vicar. 'I have not read it yet but I'm sure it will contain a word of inspiration for us all!'

He slowly unfolded the note and with everyone waiting eagerly to hear Jack's last words, he finally read out the message: 'Please vicar, you are standing on my oxygen tube!'

The vicar had just parked his old car by the roadside when a policeman approached him and asked him politely if he had reported this accident?

A headmistress asked the local vicar if he would come and speak to her girls about sex. He agreed to do this and they fixed a date. Knowing that his wife liked to scan his diary to know everything that was going on, he thought it better to make a note that he was speaking to the girls about *windsurfing*.

The vicar's wife met the head teacher soon after the appointed date and enquired how things had gone with her husband's visit. 'Oh,' said the Head, 'he was marvellous. All the girls found his talk very helpful!' The wife looked very perplexed. 'I *am* surprised,' she said. 'I didn't imagine he knew anything about it. I think he has only done it once or twice.'

A vicar searched urgently for a parking space in a busy London square but having no luck he eventually parked it in a no-parking area, leaving a note for the traffic warden: 'Have been round this square ten times without finding a parking space; forgive us our trespasses!' He signed it: 'Vicar'. When he returned after his visiting he was dismayed to find his note replaced with a ticket and another note which read: 'Have been round this square ten years. Lead us not into temptation!' It was signed: 'Traffic Warden'.

A four-year-old attended Holy Communion with her grandmother and went up to the communion rails with her for a blessing. When she got home she told her mother about it. 'Mummy, you know we went to the bit where the vicar does the cooking!'

A visitor was waiting for a bus on the Clifton Downs in Bristol, but not being sure which bus it was he consulted an aged clergyman standing by and asked if he happened to know the number. 'Yes,' said the clergyman kindly. 'Bus number 145 – the one hundred and forty-fifth bus!'

A vicar wanted a reasonably cheap holiday and decided to take his wife to Ireland where they hired a horse and caravan to take them on a gentle, leisurely tour around the countryside. The vicar was told that the horse would happily transport them in the caravan 10 miles a day. But the animal seemed to be having difficulty and on the third day refused to get up.

The vicar phoned the owner and complained: 'I thought you said it would do ten miles a day?' 'Indeed to goodness I did,' replied the owner 'but not every day.'

When Columbus started out, he didn't know where he was going. When he got there, he didn't know where he was. When he got back, he didn't know where he had been. And he did it all on other people's money. Had Columbus been a vicar he would have soon been made a bishop!

An unwed lass begins her confession to the priest. "Tis a shameful thing I have to confess Father, but I am pregnant.'
'Are you sure 'tis yours?' asks the sympathetic priest.

A little boy swallowed a 5p coin and his mother rushed with him round to the vicarage. She was greeted by the vicar's wife and cried, 'I want the vicar. I want the vicar!'
'What do you want the vicar for?' enquired the wife.
'My little boy has swallowed a coin,' explained the mother.
'You don't want the vicar,' said the vicar's wife, 'you need the doctor!'
'No, I want the vicar,' said the mother,

'everyone says the vicar can get money out of anybody!'

Seasoned travellers (vicar and wife) booking reservations at airlines counter: 'Two tickets to wherever our luggage is going.'

Man outside a church protesting to the vicar: 'I'm not going inside. They are all hypocrites in there.'
Vicar: 'Well there's always plenty of room for one more!'

A white-faced parishioner rushed to the vicarage: 'Oh vicar, the ghosts of my ancestors come and perch on the top of the fence posts all round my garden at night. What can I do?'
Tired vicar: 'Sharpen the posts of course!'

Parson visiting round his new parish meets an old man at home who has obviously been in the village a long time:
Parson: Have you lived here all your life?
Old man: Not yet!

The vicar was praising his Parochial Church Council: 'Unlike other PCCs I've known where half the council does all the work and the other half are hopeless, in this church it is completely the reverse.'

The vicar was visiting a sick man in the parish and told him he ought to call upon God. 'Well, vicar, I am so sick and lame that I just don't get out to call on anybody these days!'

The vicar was walking along the street when he met a women of the night proposing to ply her trade. He was shocked and explained that he was a vicar. He then proceeded to lecture her on the error of her ways. Troubled by her spiritual state he prayed for on his way home. The next day he met the woman again in the street.

'Oh!' he said, 'I was praying for you last night.'

'You didn't have to do that,' she replied. 'If you had just given me a ring I would have come over straight away!'

When Paddy's cat died he went to ask the priest to say a requiem mass for its soul. 'Certainly not, my dear Paddy. What ever do you think the Catholic Church is coming to, praying for cats?' Paddy approached the Anglican vicar to bury his cat and got the same response.

The priest met Paddy the next day and

asked 'Are you still trying to sort out things for
your dead cat?' 'I am that,' said Paddy. 'I even
offered the Jewish Rabbi £500 but he refused to
bury it too.' Suddenly the priest seemed to
change his attitude: 'Why didn't you tell me
the cat was a Catholic – I'll be only too pleased
to hold a requiem for it.'

A Protestant vicar met a Catholic priest and
told him he had had a dream about a Catholic
heaven.

The priest was intrigued and asked him
what it was like. 'Well,' replied the vicar, 'it
looked a nice place, with plenty of pubs, bright
music and people dancing about.'

'That's quite amazing,' replied the priest.
'Only last night I dreamt about a Protestant
heaven. It looked nice with lots of flower beds,
pretty trees and gardens.'

'And what were the people doing?' asked
the vicar?

'People? What people?' replied the priest.

A Roman Catholic priest, wanting to build a
friendly relationship with his next-door°
Church of Scotland minister, invited him to his
home for tea. On arrival, the minister was
shown into a tastefully decorated, delightfully
furnished drawing-room with fitted carpet and
fine paintings on the walls. 'Upon my word,'

remarked the Scottish divine, 'you priests certainly do well for yourselves!'

The priest answered, 'Ah yes my friend, you have the better halves but we have the better quarters!'

The vicar's son had just received a bad report from school: 'Dad, what do you think is the trouble with me? Heredity, environment or original sin?'

The priest, troubled by mice in the vestry, went to the local chemist to see if they had any poison that would kill them.

'Sorry Father! Have you tried Boots?'

'Ooh noo!' protested the priest, 'I wouldn't be wanting to kick 'em to death!'

My husband is a minister much prone to gaffes. When a guest at a wedding reception told him that Mr So-and-so was in hospital for an operation on his piles, my husband commented: 'Poor man, he *has* had a rough passage this year.'

An Irish priest was trying to sell his neighbouring Protestant minister a horse. 'Well,' said the minister, 'he looks a good animal but is he well bred?' 'Well bred!' responded the priest. 'I tell you that if this animal could talk he wouldn't speak to either of us!'

The captain made an announcement mid-air to the passengers: 'Does anybody on this aircraft know how to pray?' A clergyman raised his hand. 'Good,' said the captain. 'You start praying while the rest of us don parachutes. We are one short.'

Two men had just fitted a wall to wall carpet down in the vicarage when they noticed a bump right in the middle of the floor. Not wanting to take it up again, and believing it to be one of their discarded cigarette cartons, they started to jump up and down on it to flatten it. Mission accomplished, the vicar's wife suddenly appeared looking worried: 'Excuse me but have you seen my budgie anywhere? Its hurt its wing so it just walks round on the floor!'

Two Yorkshire farmers were discussing their respective clerics.
One said: 'Our fellow's got foot and mouth disease. 'E don't visit and 'e can't preach!'

'What a lot of friends we lose through their

borrowing money from us.
'Yes, it is touch and go with most of them.'

The graduation banquet was about to begin when the master of ceremonies was informed that the invited clergyman would not be able to attend. He quickly asked the main speaker to give the blessing. The speaker nodded, rose, bowed his head, and, in all sincerity, said, 'There being no clergyman present, let us thank God.'

A weary clergyman who had travelled to another city by train to officiate at a funeral was making his return journey when he began to suffer an acute attack of pins and needles in his foot. He turned to the old lady beside him and asked her: 'Would you mind madam if I removed my shoe, my foot's gone dead?' The lady assured him there was no problem. The clergyman felt some relief and soon fell asleep. After a little while the old lady felt obliged to nudge him: 'Excuse me, Reverend,' she said, 'but would you mind putting your shoe back on again. I think your foot's been dead some time!'

The vicar went to Israel, the church felt it was right
We bought his ticket, booked his seat, and put

him on the flight.
Now Sundays we have sermons on Jerusalem
and Dan
Archeology, the Dead Sea Scrolls, and
Paleolithic man.
We think we've learned our lesson, we've got
nothing more to fear
'Cos we are sending him to Brighton for his
holiday this year. *(Anon)*

Nervous parishioner: 'Don't drive so fast
around the corners – it frightens me.'
Vicar: 'Do as I do – shut your eyes when we
come to one.'

Jonathan, at age seven, being the youngest son
at the Vicarage, was somewhat concerned
when Mummy went back to paid employment
after several years at home. After three days of
this new experience, he came into the bed-
room at 7.30 am to find Mummy getting ready
for work and Dad still lying in bed. When
asked if he was getting used to the idea of
Mummy going out to work, he replied: 'Yes,
it's OK but what will we do if Daddy gets a
job?'

In the grim days of 1939 and 1940, notices
about National Service were posted up in
Employment Exchanges throughout Great

Britain. The official message stated that, 'All persons in the above age-groups are required to register for National Service except lunatics, the blind and Ministers of Religion.'

When churches seek a new incumbent they expect him to have, 'the strength of an eagle, the grace of a swan, the gentleness of a dove, the friendliness of a sparrow and the night hours of an owl . . . Then when they catch the bird, they expect him to live on the food of a canary.'

The vicar spotted a choirboy smoking in the churchyard and, catching him by the collar, he looked at him woefully and said: 'I see the devil has you in his grip!'
Squirming, the little lad answered back: 'Well why don't you let go then?'

The twelve-year-old accompanied his mother to the Communion rails in church to receive a blessing but as the priest did not know if the boy had been confirmed, he bent down and whispered something in his ear. Then, to the mother's consternation, the priest administered the sacrament to the boy. When his mother asked the boy later what had been said, he replied: 'Well, he asked if I was a Conservative and I said "Yes"!'

The doctor and the parson were standing with the wife beside the bed of an old man who was dying.

'I'm afraid he's gone,' said the priest.

'Yes, he has,' said the doctor.

'No, I 'aint,' murmured the patient, trying feebly to sit up.

'Lie down, dear,' said the wife, 'doctor and parson do know best.'

An evangelical vicar was asked to celebrate Holy Communion on behalf of an Anglo-catholic vicar who was sick. Unfamiliar with some of the vestments he did the best he could. Breakfasting at the vicarage afterwards he said to the vicar's wife that he hoped he got all the vestments on properly. 'Oh yes you were quite all right – except that my husband does not usually wear the book-markers!'

An evangelical clergyman was celebrating Holy Communion in an Anglo-catholic church and he had not got a clue what to wear. He arrived in the vestry to see the sacristan had laid out all the vestments ready for him. She was obviously going to have some fun watching him in his confusion knowing that he was unused to them. Not to be outdone, the visiting priest turned towards her and barked: 'Well, what are you waiting for? Vest me!'

What do you get if you cross a priest with a hyena? Mass hysteria!

Nineteen

VICARAGE VISITORS

An old tramp knocked at the rectory door asking for a small hand-out.

'I hope you won't disappoint me, ma'am,' he whined, 'but I have had no work all week, and believe me, I've asked for money, I've begged for money and now I'm crawling for money.'

'Have you thought of working for money?' suggested the rector's wife. 'Not yet, ma'am,' said the tramp. 'I am working my way through the alphabet. I've only got to 'c' so far!'

(with apologies to Best Upper Crust Jokes*)*

'Could you please give a poor bloke a bite?'

'Sorry my man, but I don't bite myself. I'll call the dog!'

'Say, vicar, would you give me £1 for a sandwich?'

'I don't know, Let me see the sandwich!'

1st comic: Every day my dog and I go for a
           tramp in the woods.
2nd comic: Does the dog enjoy it?
1st comic: Yes, but the tramp's getting a bit
           fed up.

A tramp happened to call at the vicarage asking for a handout.
The vicar responded with a question after he
had heard the usual hard luck story. 'Tell me,
my man, do you take alcoholic drinks?'
'Before I ansher that,' said the tramp, looking
puzzled, 'I musht jusht enquire if that is a
queshtion or an invitashion?'

Beggar to St Peter at the Golden Gates:
'You must be bored with your job showing
people in year after year, century after century?'
St Peter: 'You must remember, here in Heaven
things are measured differently. A million
years are but as a minute; a million pounds are
but a penny.'
Beggar: 'Could you loan me a penny. Holy
Saint?'
St Peter: 'Certainly – in a minute!'

Winston Churchill has devoted the best years
of his life to preparing his impromptu speech-
es. (F.E. Smith)

The drunk approached a policeman.
'Offisher, can you tell me where I am?'
'You are on the corner of Main Street and Market Avenue.'
'Forget the details, offisher. Whish town is it?'

A vicar was walking along the high street when he saw a man in an army greatcoat standing outside one of the main stores selling boxes of matches from a tray tied by a string around his neck. On the front of the tray hung an emotional notice: 'Please help a veteran of the Falklands War.' The vicar, being of a kindly disposition and wanting to help one of the lads who had braved the harsh conditions of war and climate in that far-off region, gave the soldier a most generous donation. The soldier, overcome by such generosity touched his cap and thanked him in a voice choking with sobs: 'Muchas Gracias, Padre.'

A medical friend was in digs in Dublin and was woken up one morning rather early and urgently by his landlady: 'Did yer heer the news this marning?' 'No,' was his rather obvious reply. 'Well, 'tis a terrible 'ting – the Holy Father woke up dead.'

(*Patient's comment about the vicar*) 'He can stay longer in an hour than most people do in a week.'

A bunch of loafers were sitting around a country store discussing the selection of a new pope, which was then in process. One old fellow listened for a while and then gave his opinion: 'Well, I think the Catholics have had it for long enough; I hope this time a Baptist gets it!'

Answering the door to two people who introduced themselves by saying, 'Good morning, we're Jehovah's Witnesses,' the white-bearded man replied, 'Good, I'm Jehovah. How are we doing?' *(Rachel Dutton)*

The vicar's wife was helping her aged mother get up the stairs on the new electric stair lift when the phone rang. From his study, the vicar was horrified to overhear his wife explaining: 'I'm sorry, dear, I'll have to ring you back. I can't talk any more just now because Mother's in the electric chair and she's just waiting for me to press the switch!'